Would You Believe...

cobwebs stop wounds bleeding?

and other **medical** marvels

Richard Platt

OXFORD
UNIVERSITY PRESS

Contents

OXFORD
UNIVERSITY PRESS

Great Clarendon Street, Oxford OX2 6DP

Oxford University Press is a department of the University of Oxford. It furthers the University's objective of excellence in research, scholarship, and education by publishing worldwide in

Oxford   New York

Auckland Cape Town Dar es Salaam Hong Kong Karachi Kuala Lumpur Madrid Melbourne Mexico City Nairobi New Delhi Shanghai Taipei Toronto

With offices in

Argentina Austria Brazil Chile Czech Republic France Greece Guatemala Hungary Italy Japan Poland Portugal Singapore South Korea Switzerland Thailand Turkey Ukraine Vietnam

Oxford is a registered trade mark of Oxford University Press in the UK and in certain other countries

Text copyright © Oxford University Press 2006

The moral rights of the author have been asserted

Database right Oxford University Press (maker)

First published in hardcover 2006

First published in paperback 2007

British Library Cataloguing in Publication Data

Data available

ISBN: 978-0-19-911497-9

1 3 5 7 9 10 8 6 4 2

Originated by Oxford University Press

Created by BOOKWORK Ltd

Printed in China by Imago

***WARNING:** The remedies and practices in this book are for information only and should not be tried at home!*

Introduction

ARE YOU FEELING WELL? Are you sure? Don't worry, the doctor will have you feeling much worse before you can say "blood transfusion". You would never hear this said in a hospital today, but in the past it was dangerously close to the truth. The story of health and healing is stranger and more scary than you might imagine.

Less than 150 years ago, doctors knew how to cure only a few of the diseases that can kill us or make our lives miserable and painful. About 250 years before that, they barely understood anything about how the human body works. And before that, medicine was little more than prayer, luck, magic and superstition.

It's easy to forget how lucky we are today. Most children born in wealthy countries will grow into healthy adults. When they get sick, medical care can usually make sure that they get well quickly and without pain. You may complain that the medicine tastes disgusting or the jab in the arm hurts, but once you find out what the sick and injured had to go through in the past, you will never complain again!

Would You Believe...?

What, why, when?

Why did the ancient Greeks study phlegm? When was the first nose-job performed? Why would a doctor drill a hole in your head? What were hares' droppings said to be good for? When were patients tied down for surgery? If you want to find out the answers, read on!

A Hole in the Head

Had you lived 12,000 or so years ago, the cure for a headache might have been a hole in the head! We don't know very much about how early people treated disease and illness, but we do know that there were some keen amateur surgeons about.

Would You Believe...?

Lucky charm
Using only stone tools, ancient surgeons scraped then drilled at the skulls of their friends. Amazingly, few of these operations killed the subjects. Most patients grew new bone over the hole. Some even carried around the cut-away bone as a charm to protect them from bad luck.

The people who performed operations thousands of years ago didn't wear white coats and masks like today's doctors. They wore animal skins and put deer antlers on their heads to make them seem important and frightening.

▲ **Trepanation tool**
Devices like this were used on battlefields in the 17th and 18th centuries to relieve the symptoms of brain injury.

▲ **True benefits**
In medieval times, trepanning was successfully used to relieve pressure on the brain and remove fragments of bone. This is still done today.

Releasing evil

Cutting a hole in the skull is known as trepanning or trephining. Archaeologists have found drilled skulls thousands of years old as far apart as France and Peru. Ancient medics relied on religion and magic for their cures, probably blaming ghosts and evil spirits for disease, pain and suffering. Experts believe that primitive doctors made holes in their patients' heads to release evil spirits from the brain.

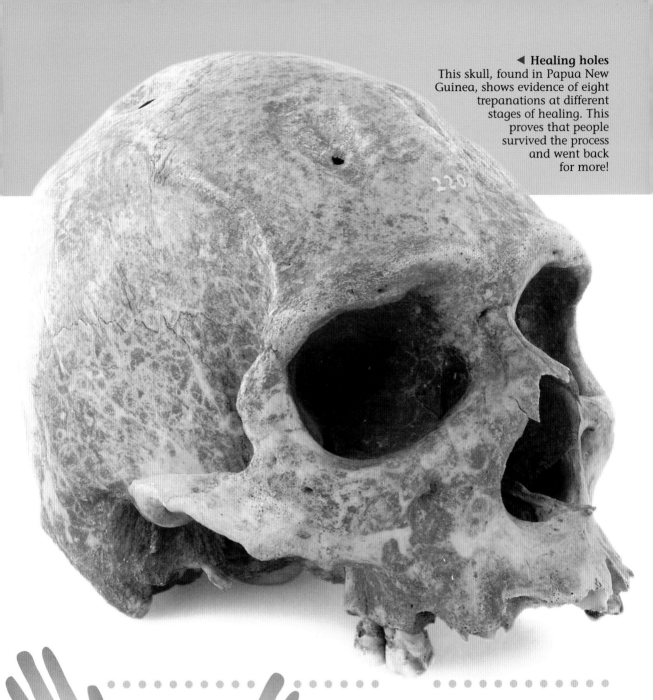

This skull, found in Papua New Guinea, shows evidence of eight trepanations at different stages of healing. This proves that people survived the process and went back for more!

Finger sacrifice

Stencil drawings in Gargas cave in southern France may be evidence of another painful, ancient cure. Drawn about 20,000 years ago, the hands have missing fingers. Some archaeologists believe that local people may have cut off a finger for a magic offering, as a way of curing a bad illness.

Ancient doctors **probably gained their patients' trust with a crafty mix of fancy dress, chanting and conjuring tricks**

Road-dust
and Writing

THE STORY OF REAL CURES and healing began some 4,000 years ago in the Middle East. The Mesopotamian people, in the land that is now Iraq, were the first to have real doctors. They still cared for their patients with a mixture of magic and medicine, but they had learned to wash and dress wounds, and operated using sharp copper knives.

To speed healing, Mesopotamian doctors used drugs, some of which had no healing effect at all. Medicines included pills made from lizard dung, but most were plants. Doctors used more than 230 plants, including fig, sesame, laurel, and apple.

The cure for a blow to the cheek was a mouthwash made from the dust of four crossroads

King's code ▶
Much of what we know about Mesopotamian medicine comes from the Code of Hammurabi. This was a list of laws made by the king of Babylon some time before 1,750BCE. It was carved on a tall stone found in the Iranian town of Susa in 1901. Some of the text on the stone says what doctors can and cannot do, and gives the punishments for those who break the law.

Scientists and sorcerers

Mesopotamia had two types of doctor – the ashipu and the asu. The asu prescribed herbal cures, while the ashipu was a spiritual healer and prescribed charms and spells to drive out the demon or god he believed was causing the disease.

Would You Believe...?

Dressing up
The Mesopotamians were the first people to use plasters, or dressings, to treat wounds. They made a paste using ingredients such as plant resin and animal fat, smeared this on the wound and kept it in place with a bandage. The paste helped to keep the wound clean and prevent infection.

The best Mesopotamian doctors grew rich from their skills. A major operation cost as much as a house. The price of failure was high, too. A surgeon who botched an operation would have his hand cut off.

Treatment included wound dressings of river mud

Clay clues ▶
Mesopotamian scribes recorded the cures of both ashipu and asu on clay tablets – showing they valued spells and herbs equally.

◀ **Healing hound**
The sitting dog was a symbol of healing in Mesopotamia. It took on special meaning 4,300 years ago when rabies, a disease spread by dog bites, struck the land.

7

Egypt's
Sunus

"**HAIL TO THE** high-priest Iry, the king's eye-doctor, shepherd to the king's bum-hole, doctor to the king's belly!" This was the official title of the most important sunu (doctor) in ancient Egypt, 4,300 years ago. His job was to cure aches, pains, wounds and illnesses everywhere on the royal body.

He was probably not very good at it. Successful cures were usually more down to luck than skill. Sunus did use herbs to heal sickness, but prayers and magic played a bigger part in treatment. This is not surprising. Egyptian doctors had little idea of how the human body worked. They could only guess at the causes of disease, and usually they just blamed evil demons.

First physician ▶
Hesy Re was the first known Egyptian doctor and dentist. There are no records of the ancient Egyptians cleaning their teeth, so he must have been a very busy man!

Pelican droppings and hippopotamus urine were among the local animal products used to make pills and ointments

Beetle power ▶
Most Egyptians could not afford the medical care that sunus offered. Instead, they protected themselves with lucky amulets like the scarab beetle, which they believed had healing and protective powers.

The sunus had more success with injuries and wounds than with diseases. The cause of an injury was obvious and it was clear whether a cure was working or not. The sunus used splints made of bark to set broken bones and help them to heal straight. They also made ointments from grease and honey, which may have worked too. Modern tests show that honey protects wounds and kills the germs that slow down or stop healing.

Secrets of the mummies

Scientists have learned about the diseases and injuries that afflicted the ancient Egyptians by studying mummies (preserved bodies) found in their tombs and pyramids. Mummies were once used as a cure themselves. Five hundred years ago, European doctors ground them up and sold them as a miracle cure for almost everything.

Cosmetic cure ▶
The funeral mask of the pharaoh Tutankhamun shows how the ancient Egyptians wore lots of eye make-up. This probably helped to protect them from eye disease. Its green and blue colours came from ground up rock that contained copper. This mineral kills the harmful germs that can infect eyes.

Healing the Greeks

Body parts ▶
Many ancient Greeks continued to turn to the gods when they became ill or were injured. They visited shrines and offered the gods a representation of the part of their body that needed healing, hoping for a cure.

RECOVERING IN ANCIENT GREECE was a pleasure, relaxing in a temple called an asklepion (named after Asklepios, the god of medicine). You put gifts for the gods on an altar, wore a blindfold and slept, dreaming that gods and snakes healed you. You awoke cured, and the gifts were gone. That was the idea, but one patient peeked: "I spotted the priest whipping cheese-cakes and figs from the holy table," he wrote.

Medicine god ▶
In Greek mythology, Asklepios was a mortal with exceptional skills in medicine and healing.

Greek temple treatments were just superstitious tricks, but by 400BCE there was something better. Hippocrates, a doctor from the island of Cos, was changing how people thought about illness. He was the first to see that it came from nature, not from the gods. He noticed that food, climate and even the work that people did affected their health. Hippocrates believed that if people ate well and rested, their bodies often healed naturally.

There's only one Hippocrates...

...Actually there may have been many! Hippocrates takes the credit for ideas that may have come from a whole group of Cos doctors. The most famous of these ideas is a promise they made to do all they could to heal the sick. Doctors today still take a version of this "Hippocratic Oath" when they finish medical school.

Medical mistakes

Not all the Greek doctors' ideas were helpful. Some thought that four bodily fluids called "humours" controlled people's health. They believed that sickness arose when there was too much of one humour, or too little of another. This was a serious mistake that held back medicine for 2,000 years.

Out of balance ▶
The four humours were phlegm (snot), blood, yellow bile and black bile. A patient's mood or symptoms helped doctors decide which humour was too strong or weak. They believed, for example, that a high fever was a result of excess blood. The treatment for this was bleeding – doctors opened their patients' veins to drain their blood.

● ● ● ● ● ● ● ● ● ● ● ● ● ● ● ● ● ●

The Greeks made syringes by tying dried animal bladders to hollow feather quills

Greek pharmacy ▶
Greek doctors knew about some of the drugs we use today, killing pain with morphine extracted from poppy sap. But they also used poisons, such as white hellebore, which would have killed more often than it cured.

Would You Believe...?

An apple a day
The ancient Greeks had great faith in the healing power of the apple – apple pulp contains a fibre called pectin, which is good for upset stomachs because it slows down the loss of water. However, the Greeks also knew what they could do with apple pips – just a quarter of a cup would kill an adult.

Oriental Wisdom

CLOSING WOUNDS WITH ants' jaws and curing disease with a thousand pin-pricks sound like very primitive treatments. But ten centuries ago, the doctors who used them in ancient India and China knew much more about sickness and health than doctors in Europe.

Indian medicine was based on a system called "Ayurveda", first written down more than 3,000 years ago. Early treatments were the usual mix of superstition and magic. However, by CE1000, Indian doctors had learned some sound lessons about disease and the human body. By practising with sharp knives on porridge-filled bags, lotus stems and watermelons, they became expert at surgery. Some even mastered cosmetic surgery and carried out the world's first nose-jobs!

The ancient Chinese created herbal cocktails as they tried to make a potion that would give everlasting life

Gory lessons

It was against the rules of the Hindu religion for Indian doctors to dissect, or cut up, dead bodies. In order to learn about the human body, they soaked corpses in water for a week. The bodies emerged so soft that the doctors could brush away the flesh to study the bones and organs inside.

◀ **A stitch in time**
Indian surgeons held up soldier ants to wounds until they gripped the edges of the wound with their pincers and pulled them together. The surgeons then snapped off the ants at the waist so that the pincers formed a neat suture, or stitch.

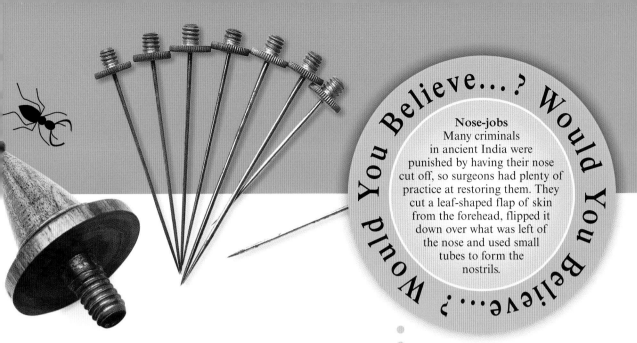

Would You Believe...?

Nose-jobs
Many criminals in ancient India were punished by having their nose cut off, so surgeons had plenty of practice at restoring them. They cut a leaf-shaped flap of skin from the forehead, flipped it down over what was left of the nose and used small tubes to form the nostrils.

Doctors in ancient China aimed to balance life forces called Yin and Yang. To do this they relied on treatments such as acupuncture – piercing the skin with fine needles – and herbal cures, both of which are still used today.

Pins and plants

Chinese doctors believed that acupuncture helped guide energy around the body, but modern research shows that the needles make the brain release pain-killing chemicals into the blood. Chinese herbal remedies are mixtures of plants. Scientists struggle to explain how they cure patients that "ordinary" medicine cannot help.

▲ **Pins and needles**
This set of Chinese acupuncture needles is about 300 years old. The needles are thicker than those used today. Most modern needles are thrown away after use to avoid infection.

▲ **Chinese surgeon**
Chinese surgeon Hua T'o (c. CE190–265) famously cut poison from the arm of general Kuan Yun while he played Go (Chinese chess) and chatted. The surgeon's skill led to his death. When a prince called on him for a headache cure, Hua T'o started trepanning (pages 4–5). The prince suspected him of plotting to kill him and had him executed.

13

Flesh of Vipers

Roman water works ▶
The Romans built long bridge-like structures called aqueducts to bring water to the city from up to 92 km (57 miles) away. Each citizen was supplied with 1,590 litres (350 gallons) of water a day – more than double that used by people in New York today.

THE PEOPLE OF ANCIENT ROME HAD no time for doctors until, 2,300 years ago, a terrible disease swept through the city. The Romans sent messengers to Greece to seek a cure, and these came back with a sacred healing snake. As their ship neared Rome, the snake slithered overboard. As if by magic, the plague vanished!

The Romans were impressed and from then on relied on Greek knowledge (or perhaps ignorance) of the human body. Most based their cures on clever ideas, rather than by looking at their patients' symptoms.

Strange ingredients

A few of the drugs the Romans used did what they were supposed to – for example, ferns that killed worms in the gut. But for many ailments Roman pharmacists mixed together lots of ingredients, most of which were useless. A popular "cure-all" contained flesh of vipers, pearls, charred stag's-horn and coral.

Would You Believe...? Would You Believe...?

Roman cures
Roman folk remedies used things that patients could easily find in the countryside: egg white for cooling sore eyes; pig dung for wounds made by iron; dog's blood for wounds made by poisoned arrows; a mouse cut in two for a snake bite; pellets of goat dung and vinegar for ulcers on the shin.

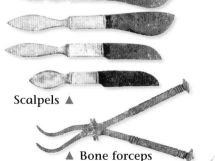

Scalpels ▲

▲ Bone forceps

◀ ▼ ▶ Soldiers and surgery
To build an empire that ruled most of Europe, Roman soldiers had to fight hard. Surgeons had plenty of work tending their wounds and they became experts at their craft. Some of the instruments used by Roman surgeons would not look out of place in a modern operating theatre.

Surgical scissors ▲

◀ **Cupping vessels for blood-letting**

Water cures

Medicine hardly improved while Rome ruled Europe, but health certainly did. There were no real doctors, but there were great engineers. They diverted clean rivers to drinking fountains and taps in the city of Rome, putting a stop to many of the diseases spread by polluted water.

◀ Gifted Galen
The most famous of all Rome's doctors was Galen. A Greek who came to Rome in CE162, Galen was a brilliant man, writing 600 books on medicine and anatomy – three before he was even a teenager. Although his studies taught Roman doctors much about the structure of the human body, he had very fixed ideas. Many were wrong, and his teachings did lasting damage. For example, his belief in the deadly process of draining sick people's blood (pages 16–17) lingered for more than 15 centuries.

Galen learned about blood flow and nerves in the human body by studying and dissecting the bodies of pigs and apes. This led to a few mistakes!

Bleeding
and Leeches

THE BEST CURE FOR disease 1,000 years ago was never to get sick! If you did, prayer was probably the most helpful treatment – there was little that a doctor could do to help you.

To identify ailments and find their cause, doctors used astrology. To help with this, a hand-written chart hung from every doctor's belt. Some of the charts showed the position of the Sun, Moon and planets, which doctors believed could affect a patient's health. Other charts gave a number to each letter of the patient's name. Doctors added them up and took away 30 to predict whether a patient would live or die.

The "cure" for almost all diseases was blood-letting

Barber-surgeons ▶
In the 14th century, doctors did not think surgery was a respectable job so they left it to barbers. One of the practices that barbers performed was blood-letting, illustrated on this wooden barber-surgeon's sign. The barbers advertised their blood-letting services by wrapping a bloody bandage round a white pole. Many barbers today still use a version of the "barber's pole", even though they can no longer cut open your veins.

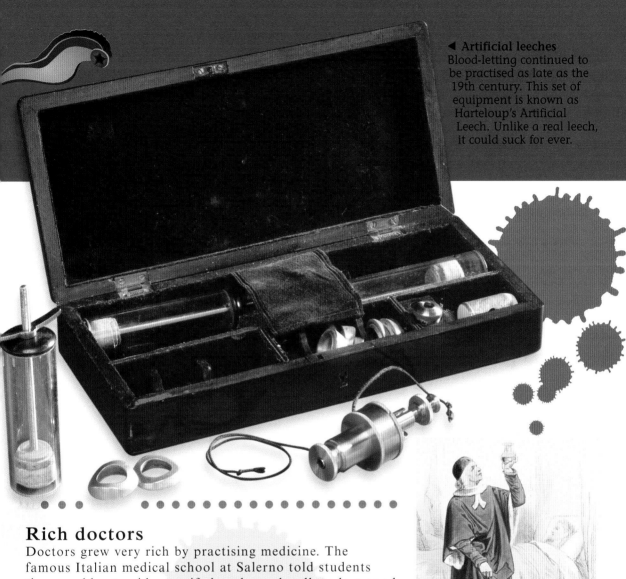

◀ **Artificial leeches**
Blood-letting continued to be practised as late as the 19th century. This set of equipment is known as Harteloup's Artificial Leech. Unlike a real leech, it could suck for ever.

Rich doctors

Doctors grew very rich by practising medicine. The famous Italian medical school at Salerno told students they would get paid more if they dressed well, rode a good horse and wore lots of rings. Before treating patients, doctors made them sign a contract agreeing to the fee – they had found that, once cured, patients forgot how sick they had been, and many refused to pay up.

The doctor opened a vein and let the patient's blood drain out – it was a treatment that could not possibly heal a patient, and killed many of them

▲ **Urine and blood**
Medieval doctors thought that studying a patient's urine was useful, and they had guidelines to follow: "Red urine which is muddy shows that the sickness is nearing the end; green urine, coming after red, is a sign of a deadly sickness; urine red like blood is a sign of a fever caused by too much blood."

17

Deadly Disease

IT DIDN'T SEEM SERIOUS AT first. Those who caught the disease just felt tired, cold and prickly to begin with, but high fever and terrible headaches followed. When a painful swelling came up in the armpit or groin, the person was bound to die – they had the plague, also known as the "Black Death" because it turned the skin dark and blotchy.

Nobody knew how the plague spread. Most blamed air pollution. To relieve "stiff" air, they rang church bells, fired guns and let birds fly round sick rooms. Religious people said that sin or scanty clothing caused it, and that children caught it as a punishment for being naughty.

▼ Untouchable
Doctors took victims' pulses with a "tickling stick" to avoid having to touch them.

▲ Burning blame
Rumours began to spread that Jews were spreading the plague, either by magic or by poisoning wells. Though the stories were obviously untrue, many people believed them and killed hundreds of Jews by burning them alive.

Doctor, doctor!
In 1720, doctors in Marseilles, France, wore a special outfit to protect themselves from the disease. The gown was leather and the eyes of the mask were glass. Some bogus, or "quack", doctors made a fortune from the plague by selling useless pills.

18

▲ **Dirty rats!**
Could the plague be so bad again? Probably not. Medical experts think that fleas living on rats spread the disease. Killing the rats or fleas stops a major outbreak, and modern drugs can cure people.

There was no real cure for the plague, but some thought tobacco stopped it. They forced schoolboys to smoke pipes or face a beating. Others believed pain would save them. They travelled from town to town whipping themselves – and spread the plague as they went.

In the worst attack, in 1349, one-third of Europe's people died

◄ **It's a cover up**
Some wealthy people carried scented herbs and flowers in a pomander. They swung the pomander to release a sweet smell to hide all the unpleasant ones they came across.

▲ **Plague posy**
The plague doctors put herbs and spices into the beak of their masks. They thought that by masking bad smells the herbs would protect them.

19

An Apple a Day

Would You Believe...?

Warts and all
There were many folk cures for warts. For example: touch each one with a different stone, put the stones in a bag and drop them on the way to church – your warts will grow on whoever picks them up; or rub your warts with meat and bury the meat – as it decays, the warts will begin to disappear.

TO CURE A STYE on the eye, rub it with your mother's wedding ring or let a dog lick it. To stop bed-wetting, eat a hare's droppings or the ash of a burned mouse. To cure mumps, put an ass's halter on the sufferer and lead them round a pig-sty three times.

Treatments like these for common diseases and problems are called folk cures or folk remedies. They sound like hocus-pocus but, less than a century ago, many people relied on them. Even today some folk remedies are still in use, especially for problems that "real" medicine cannot cure, such as baldness and back pain.

▲ **Frog fixes**
The humble frog has been used as a cure for upset stomachs, toothache, fits and piles. It is now being researched as a potential cure for HIV.

▲ **Really healing**
Many folk cures included plants that we now know contain healing chemicals. Willow, for instance, was widely used for fever. It contains aspirin, which doctors still prescribe to bring down a temperature. Some more unlikely cures work, too. Cobwebs really do stop wounds from bleeding. And sugar works as a treatment for hiccups because sugar makes muscles relax.

Hang a sock full of roast potatoes round your neck to cure a common cold

Many folk cures are nonsense, but it is easy to see why they were so popular for so long. They were cheap or free to use, so people who could not afford a doctor could treat themselves and their families for next to nothing.

Spells and superstition

Not all folk remedies involved swallowing or applying strange concoctions. In many cultures, people took a more spiritual approach to healing. Some people made use of lucky numbers; others believed in using horrible ingredients, such as dung, to disgust and drive out the evil spirit causing the illness.

Medicine man ▶
European explorers called the doctors of Asian, African and American tribes "medicine men", but these traditional healers did more than hand out cures. They were respected for their magical powers and led rituals and ceremonies, often in special masks and robes. This lion mask made a healer of the Ashanti tribe in Africa seem brave and strong.

● ●

◀ Crazy cures
Although they were not scientific, some folk remedies seemed to make sense. But others must have been difficult to believe. For example, how could cramp be cured by wearing a ring made from the hinge of a coffin?

Battlefield Breakthroughs

CUT AND STABBED, BRUISED AND beaten, warriors of the past suffered terrible wounds. For battlefield surgeons, these injuries were a rare chance to learn more about medicine and become better healers. Norwegian king Magnus the Good (1024–1047) was one of the first to look after his wounded troops. He chose the soldiers with the softest hands to treat the wounded.

The wealthy knights of 15th-century Europe took their own surgeons into battle. But centuries passed before doctors were on hand for ordinary troops.

Prepared for war ▶
Doctors in America's Civil War (1861–65) used pain-killing drugs and sterilised equipment to treat their patients.

Would You Believe...?

Paré's potions
Surgeons used to pour boiling oil into gun wounds, but it just made them worse. In 1537, Ambroise Paré (1509–1590) ran out of oil and tried rosewater, egg and turps. His patients got better, perhaps because they had not been harmed by boiling oil! He later added puppy fat, worms and oil of lilies to his mixture.

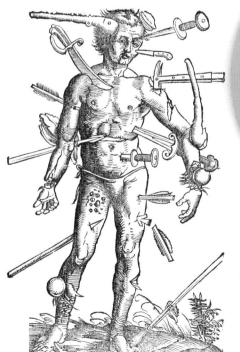

◀ Wound man
Hans von Gersdorff (1455–1529) included this gruesome picture in an instruction book he wrote in 1517 to teach surgeons how to treat battle wounds. He also gave the first exact instructions on how to amputate (cut off) wounded arms and legs, and printed recipes for soothing ointments.

Wounded soldiers were wide awake while doctors sawed off their limbs

The placebo effect

During World War II (1939–1945), doctor Henry Beecher (1904–1976) ran out of morphine, a powerful pain-killer, so he injected wounded soldiers with water. To his surprise, the worthless jab eased their pain. It worked because the soldiers expected to feel better. He named his dummy drug a "placebo" from a Latin word meaning "I shall please."

▶ **Field hospital**
Doctors in field hospitals during World War II had to work in terrible conditions. There was often little they could do to help the badly injured soldiers brought to them.

Scabs that Healed

BREATHING IN A FINE powder of ground-up scabs sounds like a horrible way to stop disease – but it works! More than 2,000 years ago, Chinese doctors were able to protect their patients against smallpox by making them sniff up scabs.

This deadly disease killed one in every ten children. Those who caught it had a high fever and horrible skin blisters. Scabs formed on the blisters after a week. It was these scabs that the Chinese healers ground up to treat healthy people.

Prepared to fight
We call this way of preventing disease inoculation or vaccination. Doctors don't do it by blowing scabs up your nose any more. They are more likely to give you an injection in the arm. This "jab" infects you with a much weakened form of the disease, called a vaccine. From it the body learns how to fight the real thing.

Queen Elizabeth I of England almost died from smallpox in 1562

Disappearing disease
Western doctors did not learn how to vaccinate people until about 1800, when Edward Jenner (1749–1823) first tried a vaccine for smallpox. Since then, vaccination for smallpox has worked so well that nobody ever catches it any more. The disease has gone forever.

▼ **Jenner's kit**
These knives were used by Jenner to extract pus from cowpox blisters.

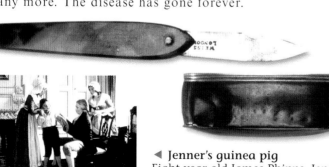

◄ **Jenner's guinea pig**
Eight-year-old James Phipps, Jenner's gardener's son, was the first to receive the new smallpox vaccine.

Smallpox blisters begin in the mouth
and spread over the entire body, even affecting
the eyes. The scars left behind are
known as pock-marks

Doctors today can protect us against many serious diseases by injecting vaccines. Children who are vaccinated can fight the diseases if they come across them later in life.

The needle protects ▶
Vaccination programmes are an essential part of aid to developing countries, which may not be able to afford the vaccines without help.

▲ Risky business
Jenner tried his smallpox vaccination after a milkmaid bragged that she couldn't catch smallpox because a cow had given her cowpox, a much less serious disease. Jenner rubbed pus from the girl's blisters into a cut in the skin of a young boy. Weeks later, he tried to infect the boy with smallpox. To his relief, the boy did not get sick.

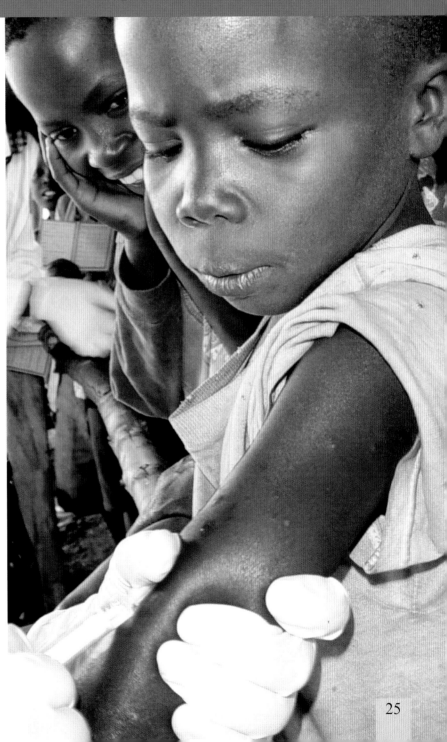

Quack, Quack

A T FESTIVALS AND FAIRS IN THE 18th century there was a show no-one wanted to miss. Squeezed in between the fire-eater and the acrobats, a quack doctor was part entertainer, part doctor – and part rogue. Quacks got their nickname because they "quacked" (boasted loudly) about their skills. They tricked people into buying "cures" that were usually useless.

A famous quack was Joanna Stephens. She managed to sell the secret of her pills to the British government for £1,600 (worth £750,000 today) – they were made from herbs, soap, eggshells and snail-shells and would not have cured anything.

Would You Believe...?

Temple of Health

Medical school drop-out James Graham was one of the most notorious "doctors" of the 18th century. He opened a clinic in London called the Temple of Health, where patients could take electric baths, be buried in warm earth, sleep in the celestial bed or be nursed by the goddesses of health.

MORRISONS PILL for EXPORTATION

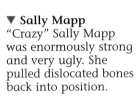

▼ Sally Mapp
"Crazy" Sally Mapp was enormously strong and very ugly. She pulled dislocated bones back into position.

Join the club
Not all quacks were cheats. A few, such as "Crazy" Sally Mapp, had real healing skills but were not considered respectable or rich enough to join the doctors' "clubs" that controlled medicine.

en las PRINCIPALES DROGUERIAS Y FARMACIAS

REUMATISMO . ARTRITIS GOTA & ARENILLAS

▲ Time reversal
Uricure pills were sold as a miracle cure for the ailments of old age, including arthritis, gout and rheumatism.

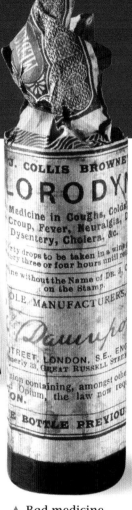

▲ Bad medicine
Dr Collis Browne's chlorodyne drops were advertised as a cure for everything from toothache to cholera. The medicine was popular in the late 1800s, but in those days they were laced with the addictive drug opium.

Gustavus Katterfelto was a quack and a conjurer. He sold a flu cure with help from two "talking" black cats and his daughter (whom he claimed to lift to the ceiling with a magnet). To announce his arrival in a town, two servants walked ahead of his carriage, blowing trumpets and handing out leaflets.

Quacks **cleverly copied the style of real** doctors **to make people** believe **their** claims **that their** pills could cure **any disease**

Germ
Warfare

I F STINKS CAUSED DISEASE AND mould appeared from nowhere, we would have a hard time staying healthy or keeping food fresh. But just 200 years ago, there were no better ways to explain sickness and rotting. Most people thought that "miasma" (bad smells) made us ill and that rot and maggots just appeared by "spontaneous generation".

The scientist who did most to prove these ideas wrong was French chemist Louis Pasteur (1822–1895). He showed that moulds did not grow in pure air. Something in the air was causing the decay. That "something" was what we now call germs or microbes (tiny beasts and plants).

▲ ▼ Animal doctor
Pasteur experimented with animal diseases. He infected cows and chickens with weakened versions of serious diseases. The animals fought off the minor infections, and this seemed to protect them against the full-blown form of the disease.

Pasteur studied yeast – a fungus that makes beer brew and bread rise

The human touch
When he began to look at human sickness, Pasteur read about Jenner and vaccination (pages 24–25). He started searching for a way to weaken diseases so that he could use them as vaccines. By 1882 he had succeeded, making vaccines to protect people against three deadly diseases – cholera, anthrax and rabies.

▲ Flasks and filters
Pasteur showed that dust in the air contains germs. He boiled some broth in a special U-shaped flask, then placed cotton wool in the neck to stop air getting in. No mould grew. But when he removed the cotton wool plug, the broth soon went mouldy.

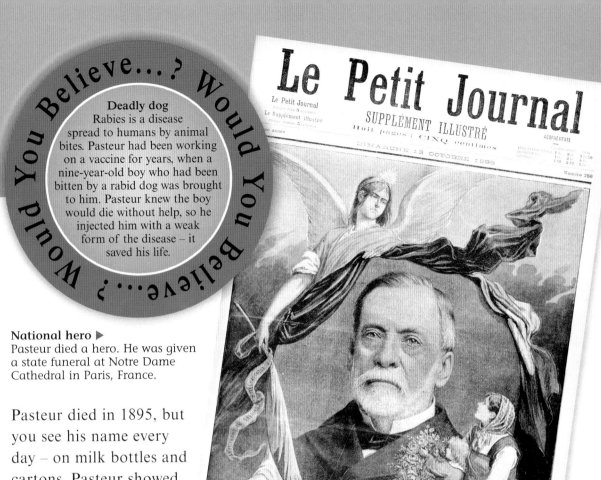

Le Petit Journal
SUPPLÉMENT ILLUSTRÉ

A LOUIS PASTEUR

National hero ▶
Pasteur died a hero. He was given a state funeral at Notre Dame Cathedral in Paris, France.

Pasteur died in 1895, but you see his name every day – on milk bottles and cartons. Pasteur showed that heating milk killed any germs it contained. This process, called pasteurisation in his honour, is still used to keep milk fresh.

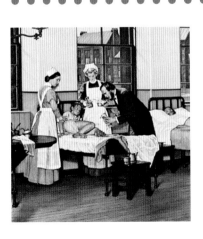

◀ **Killing germs**
When English surgeon Joseph Lister (1827–1912) heard of Pasteur's work with germs, he saw that it could save lives in the hospital where he worked. Nearly half of his patients died after surgery when their wounds went septic (rotted). Lister began cleaning wounds and spraying operating theatres with carbolic acid – a chemical that kills germs. Soon, only one in every seven of his patients was dying.

Before Lister, operating theatres were full of germs – surgeons wore ordinary clothing and no masks

Speedy Surgery

◀ **The body's pump**
Surgeons did not understand bleeding and how to stop it, until English Doctor William Harvey (1578–1657) showed, in 1628, that blood circulated round the body all the time, pumped by the heart.

I F THE IDEA OF SURGERY makes you feel weak and ill, imagine what it would be like to have an operation when you were wide awake, with nothing to dull the pain of the surgeon's knife. This is what surgery was like for most of human history. It was a terrifying ordeal. Most people agreed to it only if the alternative was death or a life in constant pain.

After the pain of surgery came the risk of infection. Without clean conditions and modern drugs, the wounds left by surgery could go septic, killing the patient.

Would You Believe...? Would You Believe...?

Born under the knife
Childbirth in ancient times was a dangerous business. When a baby was too large to pass through its mother's hips, a surgeon could cut open the mother's belly in a "caesarean" operation. This saved the baby but often killed the mother. Caesarean operations do not carry the same risk now.

▼ **Painful stones**
Doctors feared cutting into the body, but the removal of bladder stones was an exception. The constant pain caused by the crystals was so bad that patients risked surgery and its brief pain to relieve it. This instrument was used in about 1780 to reach into the bladder and grab the stones.

Painful work

Almost as frightening as the knife itself was the preparation for surgery. Patients were tied down to the operating table to keep them still. Then four strong men gripped their arms and legs. Because the pain was so dreadful, surgeons worked as quickly as they could. Some of them could saw off a patient's leg in less than a minute.

Medical school ▶
Roger of Salerno was a medieval surgeon who specialised in spinal, brain and nerve surgery. These images come from his book of surgical techniques, written in the 12th century.

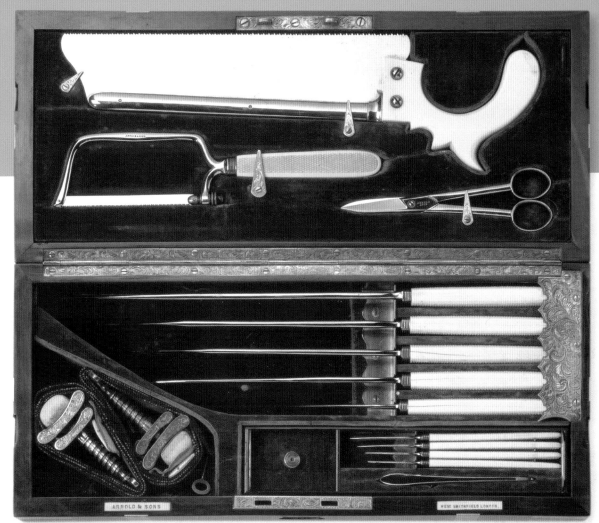

▲ **Leg lopping**
This 19th-century amputation set contains useful tools for cutting off an arm or a leg. Amputation was the most common operation and wars gave surgeons lots of practice at it: without amputation, soldiers and sailors would die from a bad wound to an arm or leg.

Most people saw a priest before they faced the surgeon's knife

Killing Pain

TO DULL THE TERRIFYING pain of surgery, patients used herbal drugs or drank alcohol until they were senseless. Nothing really took away the pain until American dentist William Morton (1819–1868) gave a remarkable demonstration at a hospital in Boston, USA, in 1846.

Morton joined a surgeon for an operation. Before surgery began, he gave the patient a chemical called ether to breathe. Within seconds, the man was fast asleep and the surgeon set to work. The audience expected the man to scream in agony, but he didn't stir.

The patient lay silent and still **as the knife cut deep into his flesh**

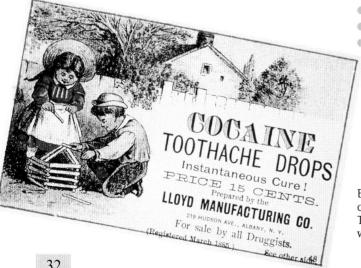

COCAINE TOOTHACHE DROPS
Instantaneous Cure!
PRICE 15 CENTS.
Prepared by the
LLOYD MANUFACTURING CO.
219 HUDSON AVE., ALBANY, N. Y.
For sale by all Druggists.
(Registered March 1885.)
See other side.

◀ Herbal painkillers
Before anaesthetics, plants like henbane, coca and cannabis were used to numb pain. The dose was critical: too little, and the pain wasn't killed; too much, and the patient was!

Medical breakthrough

Morton had demonstrated something surgeons had only dreamed of. Ether was an anaesthetic: a substance that made patients fall into a deep sleep in which they did not feel pain. His discovery changed medicine for ever.

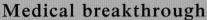

Would You Believe...?

Laughing gas
Another anaesthetic gas, nitrous oxide, came into use at about the same time as ether. It was nicknamed "laughing gas" because it made people feel drunkenly happy. One person who enjoyed nitrous oxide said that it "made you feel like the sound of a harp".

▲ **Modern anaesthetics**
Ether was safe and fairly effective, but it has since been replaced with anaesthetics that work faster and put patients into an even deeper sleep. They are injected into a patient's bloodstream or are given through a mask.

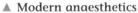

In William Morton's demonstration in Boston, the patient stayed asleep until Morton took away the ether. Then the astonished audience rushed to question him. "Did you really feel nothing?" they demanded. "Only a sensation like that of scraping with a blunt instrument," the man replied.

Vitamins and Veggies

Would You Believe...?

Scurvy cures
Scurvy became common only when European sailors began to make really long ocean journeys in the 16th century. However, a few people suffered from it even in ancient Rome and Egypt. The Egyptian cure was rather less tasty than lime juice – they used onions. The Romans preferred cabbage.

DO YOU WONDER WHAT would happen if you never ate any vegetables? Sailors in the 16th century would have told you. They ran out of vegetables soon after leaving port. After four weeks they felt weak, then their gums bled, their teeth loosened and their skin turned purple. Before they died, all their old scars opened up.

Ships' officers believed the causes of the disease, known as scurvy, included kissing girls and the bad air in the cramped decks where men slept. Remedies included burying sick sailors up to their necks in cold earth and washing the decks in vinegar. Nothing worked.

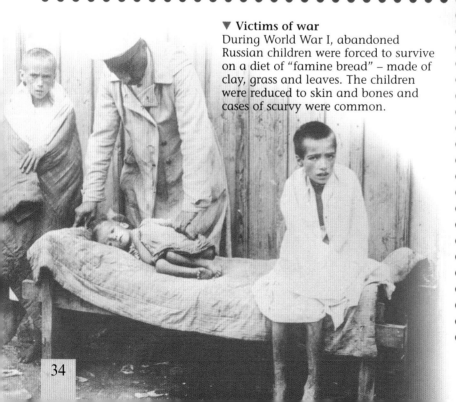

▼ **Victims of war**
During World War I, abandoned Russian children were forced to survive on a diet of "famine bread" – made of clay, grass and leaves. The children were reduced to skin and bones and cases of scurvy were common.

▲ **Getting your vitamins**
Citrus fruits like oranges, lemons and limes are high in vitamin C. One orange contains about 70mg of vitamin C – the perfect amount for keeping you scurvy-free.

Super juice

As early as 1653, a ship's surgeon suggested that a lack of fresh vegetables caused scurvy, but a century passed before anyone paid attention. Then, British admiral James Lind (1716–1794) showed that feeding sailors lime juice prevented the disease. By 1800, a disease that sometimes killed nine out of ten sailors had virtually disappeared.

▼ **Bottled up**
Fresh scurvy grass quickly
loses its vitamin content
so it was made into teas,
potions and even ale to
preserve the Vitamin C.
This scurvy-grass water
bottle dates from the 1930s.

Scurvy grass ▲
This coastal plant was eaten by
sailors returning from long voyages
to relieve the symptoms of scurvy.
Its leaves have a peppery taste
and are loaded with vitamin C.

We now know that to stay
healthy our food must
contain small amounts of
chemicals called vitamins.
It is the vitamin C in fruit
and vegetables that stops
scurvy. Since Lind's time,
scientists have found many
more vitamins and labelled
each with a letter. Learning
your food alphabet could
save you from a nasty death!

AQUA
COCHLEAR

35

Bad Water
Good Water

TURN THE TAP AND FRESH water gushes out. Clean water is vital for life, but over a billion of the world's people still can't get it. Nor could people 150 years ago. London had the worst water of any city. Sewage flowed into the Thames river, which was also the source of drinking water!

In 19th-century London, half of all children died before the age of five, most from diseases they caught by drinking sewage. Regular outbreaks of cholera, a disease spread by sewage, killed up to 14,000 Londoners in a year.

The Thames river was black and stank. Anyone falling in it died not of drowning but poisoning

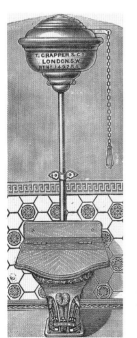

◀ **Flush and forget**
London's sewage problems were partly caused by the water closet (WC). Until people started installing this invention in the late 18th century, houses had cesspits (sewage tanks). "Night soil men" took away the solid material from these to sell to farmers as fertiliser. The WC changed this, allowing people to flush sewage straight into the river.

In the summer of 1858 the smell from the Thames was unbearable – it was called "The Great Stink". The city's law-makers ordered engineers to build sewers to carry London's filth safely away, and a separate network of pipes was built to bring in clean water for drinking from far upstream. After that, there were no more cholera outbreaks in London.

Good water

Water is no "magic cure", as people once believed, but drinking more clean water can help relieve ailments from kidney stones to constipation.

◀ Ancient water cures

Images of water spirits are carved near many mineral springs: this one is from Bath, England. Belief in the healing power of water continues to this day.

● ● ● ● ● ● ● ● ● ● ● ● ● ● ● ● ● ●

▼ Deadly pumps

Sewage seeped from the Thames into wells, killing people who drank the water from them. Dr John Snow (1813–1858) discovered that a well in Soho was spreading cholera. He had the pump handle removed so that no-one could draw water from it.

▼ Cholera kit

Doctors tried to treat cholera with medicines, but it was the discovery that it was linked to dirty drinking water that saved most lives.

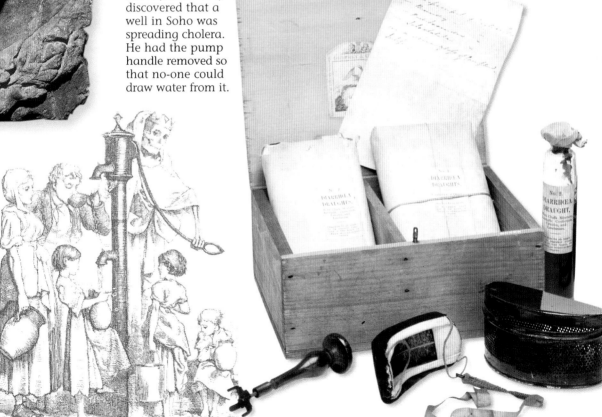

Magical Mould

Green mould ▶
Alexander Fleming noticed bacteria growing everywhere on a lab dish – except around some mould. Something in the mould was killing bacteria. He called that something penicillin.

I N A CHAOTIC WAR-TIME LABORATORY an irritable Australian scientist struggled to make mould grow. His equipment included a bathtub, milk churns, bed-pans, lemonade bottles, a bookshelf and a letter box. From this collection, Howard Florey (1898–1968) and his assistant Ernst Chain (1906–1979) made the world's first antibiotic drug, penicillin.

▲ **Fleming's lab**
Florey made penicillin after reading about the work of bacteriologist Alexander Fleming (1881–1955). Twelve years earlier, Fleming had returned from holiday to find a strange mould growing in one of his laboratory dishes. The mould had killed bacteria growing nearby. Fleming realised that his discovery was important, but he stopped work on it when he failed to turn the mould into a useful drug.

Florey and Chain tried out their drug in February 1941 on a dying policeman. With each dose, he got a bit better but they did not have enough to cure him. To make more, they collected his urine and extracted the penicillin that had passed through his body. The policeman died, but Florey and Chain made more penicillin, tried again – and cured eight people.

In 1945, Fleming, Florey and Chain shared medicine's greatest award – a Nobel Prize – for the discovery of penicillin and its effect

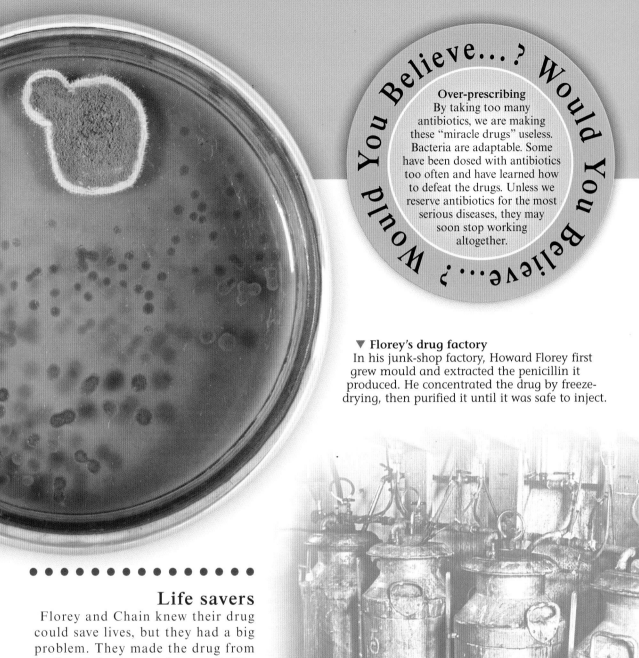

Would You Believe...?

Over-prescribing
By taking too many antibiotics, we are making these "miracle drugs" useless. Bacteria are adaptable. Some have been dosed with antibiotics too often and have learned how to defeat the drugs. Unless we reserve antibiotics for the most serious diseases, they may soon stop working altogether.

▼ **Florey's drug factory**
In his junk-shop factory, Howard Florey first grew mould and extracted the penicillin it produced. He concentrated the drug by freeze-drying, then purified it until it was safe to inject.

Life savers

Florey and Chain knew their drug could save lives, but they had a big problem. They made the drug from the liquid that oozed from penicillin mould, and it took a bathtub of liquid to make one drop of the drug. They went to the USA for help. There, scientists worked out how to grow the mould more quickly – on slices of melon! By the time World War II ended, there was enough penicillin to treat all the wounded soldiers from Britain, the USA and their allies. Antibiotics have since saved millions more lives.

Mad
or Bad?

ENTALLY ILL patients may look normal and seem healthy, but they are as sick as someone with a rash, a fever or a gaping wound. Today, drugs and therapy can help them get well, but for much of history the only treatment was exorcism – a religious ceremony designed to get rid of the "demons" people thought caused the "madness".

Most mentally ill patients got no treatment at all. They were chained up as "idiots" or "lunatics" in mad-houses such as London's Bethlehem Hospital. Mad-houses were visitor attractions – anyone who could afford the entrance fee could go and stare at the terrified inmates.

▼ The mad-house
Today, any scene of mad confusion is described as "bedlam". The word comes from the shortened name of the most famous mad-house, London's Bethlehem Hospital. It started taking in mentally ill people in 1377. They were chained up, often naked, and punished for violence by being ducked in cold water or whipped.

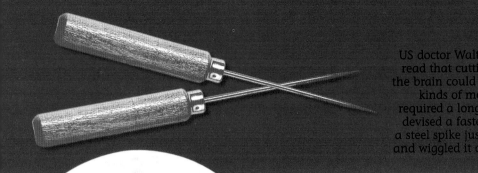

US doctor Walter Freeman (1895–1972) read that cutting nerves at the front of the brain could help people with certain kinds of mental illness. The surgery required a long operation, but Freeman devised a faster method. He banged in a steel spike just above the patient's eye and wiggled it about to mash the brain.

Serious treatment of mental illness began in the 19th century, but this did not entirely stop the cruelty. As late as 1950, doctors were "operating" on the brains of the mentally ill with iron spikes and hammers. This crude surgery, called lobotomy, caused terrible brain damage.

Some children were lobotomised for being disobedient or getting a bad school report

▲ **Lunatics**
People once believed that a full moon made mental illness worse. They called the illness lunacy and its sufferers lunatics, from the Latin name for the moon – *lunaris*.

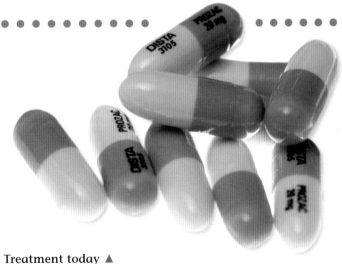

Treatment today ▲
Fortunately, treatment of mental illness today is kinder and works better than in the past. Mind-altering drugs, first used in the 1950s, can cure patients with some forms of mental illness. Drugs can make seriously ill patients feel better and help them to lead normal lives.

Shocking Discoveries

▼ **Defibrillator**
Used scientifically, electricity saves lives. This modern defibrillator machine shocks heart attack victims, to get their hearts beating again.

WHEN SCIENTISTS first began studying electricity, they believed that this invisible force would unlock many of the mysteries of medicine. After all, in one of the first electrical discoveries, Italian Luigi Galvani (1737–1798) made a frog's leg twitch by passing electricity through it.

In later experiments, scientists amazed audiences by creating huge sparks like lightning. Surely anything with such power must affect the body?

Body electric

People in the 19th century were impressed by the magnets, sparks and health claims and rushed to buy "electro-therapy" machines. At best, these devices gave patients a harmless, tingling electric shock. But some, such as "electric belts" and "electric corsets", did nothing. The "therapy" was no more than a trick for taking money from people who imagined they were ill.

Medical electric machine ▶
Like hundreds of similar "medical electrical" machines, this one delivered an impressive but useless shock to anyone gripping the handles.

42

THE "VERY THING" FOR LADIES
FOR AN ELEGANT FIGURE & GOOD HEALTH.
HARNESS' ELECTRIC CORSETS
PRICE ONLY 5/6 POST FREE.

FOR WOMEN OF ALL AGES.

THEY CURE WEAK BACK

HARNESS' ELECTRIC CORSETS
ONLY 5/6 POST FREE
By wearing these perfectly designed Corsets the most awkward figure becomes graceful and elegant, the internal organs are speedily strengthened,
THE CHEST IS AIDED IN ITS HEALTHY DEVELOPMENT
And the entire system is invigorated.
Send at once Postal Order or Cheque for 5s. 6d. to the Secretary, C Dept.
THE MEDICAL BATTERY CO. LIMITED.
52, OXFORD St. LONDON. W.
ONLY 5/6 POST FREE

▲ **Electric corset**
Lined with wires, the electric corset was said to cure kidney, liver and bladder troubles and backache. Curiously, women felt no sensation – perhaps because it was doing nothing.

We now understand more about electricity in our bodies. We know that electrical currents flowing in our nerves allow us to feel pain and move our muscles, and that our thoughts are really flashes of electrical power.

The sparks and cracks of electricity made it the perfect quack cure

Back to the Age of Ignorance

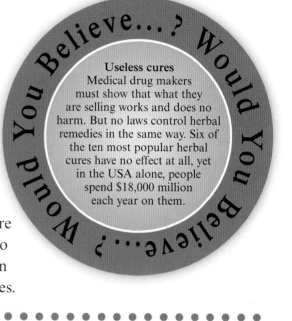

MODERN MEDICINE can do amazing things. It can protect us from diseases that would once have killed us in days, and surgeons can save our lives by giving us a new heart or kidneys. Smart drugs can even deliver cures that are personally tailored to each of us.

But doctors still cannot cure everything, and growing numbers of their desperate patients are turning to the past for a cure. Even people who have diseases that are easily cured with modern drugs are using fashionable alternative remedies.

Would You Believe...? Would You Believe...?

Useless cures
Medical drug makers must show that what they are selling works and does no harm. But no laws control herbal remedies in the same way. Six of the ten most popular herbal cures have no effect at all, yet in the USA alone, people spend $18,000 million each year on them.

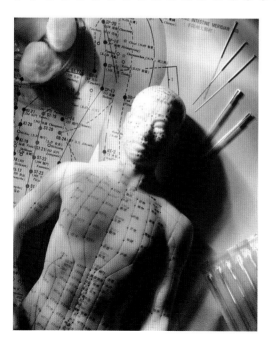

◄ **Acupuncture**
Brain scans of treated patients show that the ancient Chinese needle-prick treatment really does cure pain for some people, although Western doctors don't know exactly why or how.

Looking forwards
Some alternative remedies work, even if scientists cannot explain why, but many do not. They come from a time when guesswork, star-signs, religion and superstition were the only cures for the sick. By turning away from modern medical knowledge, we throw away a thousand years of progress.

Some alternative remedies **have brought back the** tricks **of the 18th-century** quacks

Find out More

You can find out lots more about the history of medicine from these websites and places to visit.

Websites

Learning from the past
www.schoolscience.co.uk/content/4/biology/abpi/history/
An interactive timeline of medicine, from trepanning to the present day.

Doctor over time
www.pbs.org/wgbh/aso/tryit/doctor/#
This website from the United States Public Broadcasting Service shows how doctors from the past treated different ailments.

Dream Anatomy
www.nlm.nih.gov/exhibition/dreamanatomy
An introduction to how people have drawn and painted the organs, muscles and bones of the human body, from the United States National Library of Medicine.

Smallpox
www.nlm.nih.gov/exhibition/smallpox
This site tells the story of a killer disease and how it was wiped out for ever.

Kidswork
www.knowitall.org/kidswork/hospital/
Find out about medicine from the past and learn what goes on in today's hospitals.

Places to visit

Alexander Fleming Laboratory Museum
St Mary's Hospital, Praed Street
London W3 8BB
Telephone: 0207 886 6528
Web page: www.stmarys.nhs.uk/about/fleming_museum.htm
Here you can see a reconstruction of Alexander Fleming's laboratory – exactly as it was in 1928.

Anaesthesia Heritage Centre
21 Portland Place
London W1B 1PY
Telephone: 020 7631 1650 extension 8806
Web page: www.aagbi.org/heritage_museum.html
In the museum of Britain's Association of Anaesthetists, you can see objects from the history of painless surgery from 1774 to the present day.

Wellcome Trust
This is an independent charity funding research to improve human and animal health. The Wellcome Trust does not have its own museum that is open to the public, but it stages exhibitions at other places. You can see a listing of these on the Website: www.wellcome.ac.uk/whatson/exhibitions/
The vast website covers many medical topics, but is mainly intended for adults.

The Old Operating Theatre
9A St Thomas' Street
London SE1 9RY
Telephone: 020 7378 8383
Website: www.thegarret.org.uk/oot.htm
This extraordinary old operating theatre is in the attic of a church. Until the mid 19th century, medical students filled its horseshoe-shaped stands to watch their teachers carry out surgery on wide-awake patients. There is also a museum and a herb garret where pharmacists prepared herbal cures.

Florence Nightingale Museum
2 Lambeth Palace Road
London SE1 7EW
Telephone: 020 7620 0374
Website: www.florence-nightingale.co.uk/
A museum devoted to the life of Britain's most famous nurse, Florence Nightingale.

The Hunterian Museum
The Royal College of Surgeons
35-43 Lincoln's Inn Fields
London WC2A 3PE
Telephone: 020 7869 6560
Website: www.rcseng.ac.uk/museums/galleries/
The museum tells the story of surgery from the time when barbers lopped off limbs, through to the present day.

Glossary

Many of the medical terms used in this book are explained on this page. Where a word is in italics, it means the word has its own entry.

acupuncture
Chinese therapy that involves inserting fine needles into the patient's skin.

amputation
Cutting off part of the body, such as an arm or a leg.

anaesthetic
Chemical that stops a patient feeling pain.

antibiotic
Group of *drugs* that kill *bacteria*.

bacteria
Smallest of living creatures, some of which cause *disease* in humans, animals and plants.

blood-letting
Opening a vein to let blood flow out, in the mistaken belief that this will cure illness.

cholera
Deadly *disease* of the gut, spread by polluted water.

disease
Unhealthy disturbance to the body, often caused by an *infection*, poisons or a weakness passed on from the sick person's parents.

dissection
Cutting up a dead body in order to study its structure.

drug
Chemical used to cure illness.

electro-therapy
Treatment that uses electricity.

ether
Anaesthetic liquid, the vapour of which sends those who breathe it into a deep sleep.

fever
Higher-than-normal body temperature caused by illness.

germ
Tiny plant or animal that can cause illness.

humours
Four fluids that people once believed kept the body healthy if they were all present in the right quantities.

infection
Invasion of the body by *germs*, often causing *disease*.

lobotomy
Cutting off part of the brain.

lunatic
Name once (but no longer) used for any mentally ill person.

nerve
Thread-like flesh that carries the electrical signals that let us move or sense what's around us.

operation
Treatment in which a *surgeon* cuts open the body to treat a *diseased* or damaged part.

pasteurisation
Heating food or drink to kill the *germs* that might spoil it.

penicillin
First *antibiotic*, made from mould.

pharmacist
Someone expert in the use or the making of *drugs*.

placebo
Treatment with no curative effect that a patient mistakenly believes will heal them.

plague
Name for *diseases* that spread quickly, killing many people.

rabies
Deadly *disease* spread by the bites of dogs and other animals.

scurvy
Disease caused by the lack of *vitamin* C, which is found in fresh fruit and vegetables.

septic
Rotting

surgeon
Doctor expert in cutting open the body to cure illness inside it.

trepanation
Drilling a hole in the head.

vaccination
Protecting someone against a *disease* by *infecting* them with a weakened form of it.

vitamin
Chemical essential to health, found in small amounts in food.

Index

Picture credits

The publisher would like to thank the following for their kind permission to reproduce their photographs:

Position key: c=centre; b=bottom; l=left; r=right; t=top

Cover: Front: tr: K-Photos/Alamy; cr: Medical-on-Line/Alamy; bl: Wellcome Library, London; tl: Gusto/Science Photo Library. Back: br: OUP/Photodisc; bl: OUP/Ingram

1: NHPA/James Carmichael Jr; 4c: Musée d'Histoire de la Medecine, Paris, Archives Charmet/Bridgeman Art Library; 4tr: Bettmann/Corbis; 5t: Wellcome Library, London; 6cl: Bookwork/Darren Sawyer; 6r: Art Media/Heritage-Images; 7l: The British Museum/Heritage-Images; 8bc: TopFoto.co.uk Werner Forman Archive; 8–9b: Bookwork/Darren Sawyer; 9r: Sandro Vannini/Corbis; 10cl: Mary Evans Picture Library; 10–11c: The British Museum/Heritage-Images; 12b: Michael & Patricia Fogden/Minden Pictures/FLPA; 13l: © Copyright the Trustees of The British Museum; 13r: Wellcome Library, London; 14bl, 14bc, 14br: Courtesy of Historical Collections & Services, Claude Moore Health Sciences Library, University of Virginia; 15b: Mary Evans Picture Library; 15t: Vanni Archive/Corbis; 16: Science Museum/ Science & Society Picture Library; 17cr: Science Museum Pictorial/Science & Society Picture Library; 17t: Science Museum/ Science & Society Picture Library; 18bl: Christel Gerstenberg/ Corbis;

18r: Bettmann/Corbis; 19bl: Bookwork/Darren Sawyer; 19c: Private Collection/Bridgeman Art Library; 20r: NHPA/James Carmichael Jr; 21r: TopFoto.co.uk Fortean 1933/ERG; 22bl: Wellcome Library, London; 22–23t: Tria Giovan/Corbis; 23br: University of Virginia Visual History Collection, Special Collections, University of Virginia Library; 24bl: Courtesy Pfizer Inc; 24bc, 24br: Science Museum/ Science & Society Picture Library; 24–25c: Science Museum/Science & Society Picture Library; 25r: Jean Pierre Aim Harerimana/ Reuters/Corbis; 26: Wellcome Library, London; 27tc: Wellcome Library, London; 27tr: Science Museum/Science & Society Picture Library; 28b: Science Museum/Science & Society Picture Library; 29bl: Courtesy Pfizer Inc; 29tr: Oxford Science Archive/Heritage-Images; 30–31b: Ann Ronan Picture Library/Heritage-Images; 30–31c: Science Museum/Science & Society Picture Library; 31t: Science Museum/Science & Society Picture Library; 32bl: Corbis; 32–33c: Science Museum/Science & Society Picture Library; 33tr: Pete Saloutos/Corbis; 34b: Bettmann/Corbis; 34tr, 35tl: Bookwork/Darren Sawyer; 35r: Wellcome Library, London; 35tc: TH Foto-Werbung/Science Photo Library; 36bl: Bettmann/Corbis; 36–37tc: Ann Ronan Picture Library/ Heritage-Images; 37br: Science Museum/Science & Society Picture Library; 38cl: Wellcome Photo Library; 39tl: The British Library/Heritage-Images; 39br: Wellcome Library, London; 40–41b: Wellcome Library, London; 41br: Najlah Feanny/Corbis; 41cl: NASA; 41t: Wellcome Library, London; 42t: Sotiris Zafeiris; 42–43c: Science Museum/Science & Society Picture Library; 43tr: Mary Evans Picture Library; 44bl: William Whitehurst/Corbis